ALPHABESTIARY

ALPHABESTIARY

A POETRY~EMBLEM BOOK

H. Masud Taj and Bruce Meyer

EXILE
editions

Library and Archives Canada Cataloguing in Publication

Taj, H. Masud, 1956-
    Alphabestiary : a poetry-emblem book / H. Masud Taj, Bruce Meyer.

ISBN 978-1-55096-249-9

    I. Meyer, Bruce, 1957- II. Title.

PS8639.A365A65 2011   C811'.6   C2011-906329-8

Introduction and A-Z Poetry Copyright © H. Masud Taj, 2011
Introduction and A-Z Text Copyright © Bruce Meyer, 2011
Videos and QR Copyright © Michael Callaghan, 2011

Design and Composition by Digital ReproSet mc
Typeset in Papyrus and Book Antigua at the Moons of Jupiter Studios
Printed by Imprimerie Gauvin

The publisher would like to acknowledge the financial assistance of
the Canada Council for the Arts and the Ontario Arts Council, which
is an agency of the Government of Ontario.

 Conseil des Arts **Canada Council**
du Canada   for the Arts

 ONTARIO ARTS COUNCIL
CONSEIL DES ARTS DE L'ONTARIO

Printed and Bound in Canada in 2011
Published by Exile Editions Ltd.
144483 Southgate Road 14 – GD
Holstein, Ontario, N0G 2A0

Canadian Sales Distribution: U.S. Sales Distribution:
McArthur & Company   Independent Publishers Group
c/o Harper Collins   814 North Franklin Street
1995 Markham Road   Chicago, IL 60610
Toronto, ON M1B 5M8   www.ipgbook.com
toll free: 1 800 387 0117   toll free: 1 800 888 4741

This book is for Zeba and Kerry,
Noah, Katie and Zahra,
and their grandparents.

Contents

play time 2:26

QR codes/video features appearing in the book:

H. Masud Taj: Calligraphy (page viii)
The author, as a calligrapher, inscribes the animals that appear in the book..
   http://tinyurl.com/Alphabestiary-pg-viii

Bruce Meyer and H. Masud Taj: Future, Present, Past (page 13)
The authors discuss how the QR code completes an evolutionary cycle for the printed book.
   http://tinyurl.com/Alphabestiary-pg-13

Bruce Meyer: The Funny Bunny Factory and Animals in Literature (page 16)
The author discusses the importance of animals in literature.
   http://tinyurl.com/Alphabestiary-pg-16

H. Masud Taj: Dragonfly (page 30)
The author explains the origin of his animal poems.
   http://tinyurl.com/Alphabestiary-pg-30

H. Masud Taj: Urdu (page 32)
The author recites a poem of his ancestor in Urdu.
   http://tinyurl.com/Alphabestiary-pg-32

Bruce Meyer and H. Masud Taj: Dragon (page 44)
The authors recite their Dragon pieces.
   http://tinyurl.com/Alphabestiary-pg-44

The video links featured in this book are also available online at the above URLs.

God, His angels and all those in heavens and on earth, even ants in their hills and fish in the water call down blessings on those who teach others beneficial knowledge.

—The Hadith (Al-Tirmidhi No. 1392)

And God created Great whales, and every living creature that moveth, which the waters brought forth abundantly, after their kind, every winged fowl after his kind: and God saw that it was good.

—The Bible (Genesis 1:21)

PAST, PRESENT, FUTURE
AN EDITORIAL NOTE FROM THE PUBLISHER

When pictures first appeared in books, they were placed on the page to push the written word into the realm of animated ideas. Pictures in illuminated manuscripts, woodcuts in Renaissance books, and copperplate etchings in eighteenth-century volumes were attempts to make books speak to us through the power of the visual. This new presentation provided a completeness through a sense of gravity and grace.

Today, and more so in the future, one will find QR codes taking their important place on products, offering the consumer an added experience: watch a Peruvian family making the shoes now in your hand at the store; see an artist at work in her studio while completing the work you are admiring in a gallery; see how the printed page can be but one aspect of publishing as the book, computer, and telephone converge to provide a fuller, more enriched "reading" experience.

Alphabestiary is a part of this evolution, for it enables the book not only to be read and imagined, but through a form of ascendancy, to talk back to the reader through video shorts, featuring author readings from the text, author discussions on the writing process, and their insights into the creative process.

play time 4:51

After all, books should come alive. This is a volume that celebrates living things. *It is now alive in your hands!*

Note: in the book you will find QR codes placed alongside complementary text: scan these with your smartphone. This will download a video, and then you can enjoy the added feature.

(Scanning and reading apps are readily available online, some free, others for a fee; if you don't already have them, you'll need to search, download and install.)

FOREWORD

This book represents a meeting of worlds: animal and human, poetry and prose, oral literature and scholarly exegesis, and ultimately of East and West. As the pages of this book face into each other and become one single volume, we hope that the readers will recognize the spirit of alterity between two poets who face each other interculturally just as *homo sapiens* interfaces with animal species in a world that has no boundaries, no divisions and, ultimately, no East and no West. That unified world is the small space of this planet that we share with the animals that have spoken to both of us throughout our lives. This volume is a celebration not only of a meeting of two individuals, cultures and literatures – a too rare event where East meets West with joy and delight – but of the animals we have praised and probed through our words. Those creatures live in our imaginations as much as they live with us on this tiny blue planet.

H. Masud Taj and Bruce Meyer, June 2011

An Introduction by Bruce Meyer

Most of us can recall, in the haziness of our first memories, those tiny books that made their ways into our cribs, high chairs, or toy boxes. In many cases, those books were about animals, or the alphabet, or both. Beneath their bright colours and their cartoon critters, there was something beautifully innocent about them. They were our first glimpses into the world of the printed word. Some had squeakers in the pages or made a mooing sound when the pictures were pressed. They were meant to astonish in a very simple way. They were also meant to tell us stories about the letters of the alphabet or the animals in the pictures with the intent that we would make a connection between what existed on the page and what lived in the world around us.

Those first books were anomalies because they gave us the twenty-six essential elements of written language long before we could read. As benchmarks in the *terra incognita* of reality, such little volumes attempted to orient us to the world of things, creatures, sounds, shapes, ideas and information. Although it is impossible to remember how we reacted, to watch a child turn the pages of such a book is to witness the unfolding of a mystery that we were part of. Of all the books that come and go throughout our lives, these little alphabet books are the ones that rarely survive long enough for us to revisit them as artefacts of our pre-literate selves. Like our memories of the times we read them, most are lost. Some ended up as stand-ins for teething rings. Many were tossed out or sold to pregnant mothers at garage sales. One child I know ate her first book, and I tease her that she reminds me of St. John on Patmos when he either figuratively or literally devoured the Gospels. There is a Dürer woodcut that portrays the saint eating a book. Growing up, I continually heard the phrase "books are good for you." Wherever they find their final resting place, the one thing that can be said about books is that they sustain us in many ways.

play time 2:58

The point is that from the very start of our literate lives, books sustain us, one way or another. They feed us from the great table of knowledge and help to connect us to the world we live in. That world, as we are reminded whenever creatures poke their heads into our bubbles of daily life, is also populated by animals that are born, grow, and develop reactions to the world we share with them.

The other wonderful thing that books and the written word do for us is that they bring us together, connecting us with their content, with imaginary and real worlds that we take into our minds and vicariously experience through the power of the written world. Through the connective power of books and the written world, there is ultimately no east or west to our globe, but a single place we all inhabit and share with nature. That is how this book began.

In the summer of 1998, I received an email from someone in India who sent me his analysis of my poems that he had come across on the web. I was, at the time, in the midst of a very demanding administrative job at the University of Toronto. I hit reply and asked, "Who are you?" I used to get upwards of sixty emails each morning, both internal and external, and I was obliged to answer them all thoroughly. In reply, the Indian poet sent me "Killing and the Art of Calligraphy." It was his 1991 villanelle. At that time I was deeply into the New Formalist movement that was at its height in the United States. Villanelles were something for which I had a passion. I wrote back and told him I liked it and sent him one of mine, "The Ferry to South Baymouth." The next email contained a 1986 Petrarchan sonnet "Hagia Sophia." We discussed the question the American poet Alfred Corn had posed to me at the West Chester Conference about whether the Petrarchan sonnet could handle narrative and I sent him "Ithaca." Here was someone, I decided, who knew something about poetry. What I discovered about his work was that it was not mere finger painting with words but a rich dialogue between poet and reader that was carried through thought, consideration, reconsideration, and depth of idea. His works were exquisite pieces of verbal architecture.

Those emails began the correspondence and the friendship between Masud Taj and me. He told me that he was an oral poet who was also a practicing architect in Mumbai in India. Those were pre-Google days, but he had found my work while surfing the net. "Send me more of your poems," I told him one day. "I liked the ones I saw." "Sorry," came the response, "the rest are oral poems and are not written down." I kept writing to him, urging him to write them down. "If I did that, they would not be oral poems." He had a point. A poet has to be true to his voice and if the voice isn't aimed at the paper, then the question arises as to whether it should live there permanently.

Oral poetry resides at the roots of all literary culture. A poem has to be heard, not just read. Homer's epics were originally sung. They were intended to be performance pieces. Those who performed them, at least in the Western tradition, were called *rhapsodes*. Plato takes apart a *rhapsode* for twisting Homer's ideas in the Platonic dialogue, *Ion*. The problem with oral poetry, as Bernard Knox points out in his introduction to Robert Fagles' translation of the *Iliad*, is that it is constantly in a state of mutation. The performer looks around his recital hall as he carries the story in the rhythm and tune of his prolonged song and cannot see bronze weapons. He sees iron weapons instead, so the newest version of the struggle on the plains of Ilium is about Greeks and Trojans feeling the slice and stab of iron rather than bronze. The next poet to perform the poem, who learns from the previous poet, only knows about steel blades and spearheads. Because oral poems rely on memory (and according to David Hume we cannot trust our memories because they are subject to all sorts of mutabilities, pressures, and filters), they alter from teller to teller and from recollection to recollection. The *Beowulf* that we know as an epic may be greatly different from the Beowulf that was told by an early bard. But of all the forms in which we encounter literature, oral poetry is, perhaps, the frailest because it is so mutable and, because it travels by word of mouth, it lives in the same general neighbourhood of factuality as rumours do. "Write them down, Taj," I insisted in my emails. "Write them down or they will simply vanish into thin air."

What has been so evident in our friendship over the years has been the fact that we are two individuals, dedicated to poetry and to the idea of sharing our knowledge with one another – an East meets West relationship that gives me hope that the rest of the world will sit down and talk and learn from one another and experience the wonder that comes from an exchange of perspectives. That exchange grew beyond emails one day when Taj messaged me to say that he was immigrating to Canada. Not long after he arrived in 1999, we arranged to meet for the first time and put faces to the names and voices that had emerged from our electronic correspondence. When we finally met at my Toronto home, Taj presented me with a framed calligraphic version of his poem "Owl." What impressed me about his calligraphy was the flow of the letters, the way they seemed to take flight as if they were part bird and part light, waiting to lift off the page into the sky. I placed the poem in its frame in my dining room, and it remains a fixture of that room.

To celebrate his arrival, I arranged for Taj to give a reading in the Hart House Library at the University of Toronto, an august place to commence a Canadian literary presence. I remember that the audience sat spellbound as he recited his poems, some of which appear in this book. The inevitable question came from the rapt audience at the end of the reading: where can we get your poems? They all had startled looks on their faces when he said, "You have them already. They are in your minds."

Eventually, Taj gave in to my incessant and irritating demands and did write them down. In the spring of 2009, he dropped by for a visit to my new home in Barrie. He had settled in Ottawa and was visiting family members in Ajax. As we sat in the living room, he presented me with of one of my poems in his beautiful calligraphy. The lines read "they disappeared in their mother tongue / a whisper in the night of heaven." The poem was "Subtitles." I had dedicated it to Taj in my 2000 collection, *Anywhere*. He also showed me an artist's monograph that featured his poems. I started reading through his manuscript, and not being a good host I paid more attention to his words than to him as a guest. It was shameful of me. I read "Lion." Immediately, the critic and literary scholar kicked in as the age-old question "what does this remind of" began to play in my mind. I described how he had evoked the richness of the idea of the lion, its kingly state, its pervasiveness in English art and literature as a symbol for power, tradition, regal heritage and the British Empire. I suspect I went on a bit. Taj looked me in the eye and said, "Bruce, you really should write that down."

"It is just the sort of thing I would say to my students if we encountered a lion in a poem or short story."

"You really should write that down," he repeated.

When he returned to Ottawa, Taj mentioned my impromptu criticism *ad hoc* to a local poet he knew there, Sean Moreland. Sean, who is also a critic, was impressed by the lucidity of what I had said (though, as someone who often says too much, I had trouble remembering the nuances of what I had said – the words escaped me but not the ideas). Taj conveyed to me in an email that Sean had suggested that a dialogue of this kind would make for a very unique book. I agreed. That was the first inkling of *Alphabestiary*.

I had no idea where this dialogue would lead. I poured over Taj's poems and assembled my own thoughts about the animals. I took his manuscript up to the quiet environs of Manitoulin Island so I could hear his voice in the poems through the silence of a Northern summer. Some of my reactions to the poems pointed me towards general ideas about the importance of symbols and iconography in English and European literature. Taj's animals each project their own personality, their own sense of self-awareness, and their own unique identity. That is what symbols do: they speak for themselves as well as for a myriad of ideas and suggestions. Some animals in Taj's menagerie evoked personal memories that turned me towards biographical asides.

I thought, Where have I seen this sort of reaction to a text before?

The answer lay in Medieval literature of the scholastic tradition where the monks of such inhospitable places as Lindisfarne and Glastonbury and Oxford sat in cold scriptoriums where they copied the reactions of leading authorities on the Bible from one sheet of velum to the next. Their underfed bodies drove their minds to flights of fancy in both decorative expression and in the editorializing and commentary they slipped by the Abbots in the margins – fingerprints of personalities that would otherwise be lost to time. As an English professor, the strength of my trade resides in the margins of the books I teach, where I scribble my thoughts and reactions to the text and organize my lectures around the codes of marginalia I create. At that moment, I realized that a good portion of my life was spent reiterating the ancient art of exegesis that is practiced in both the East and the West, and that exegesis – the serious yet playful, reactive, commentative kind – was, in itself, a neglected form of literature. There was still no outlet for this dialogue of prose and poetry. That's where Michael Callaghan, the publisher of Exile Editions, entered the picture.

"We'd love to see something that is a mixture of poetry and prose," he said one evening during a telephone conversation. As he said it, I had no idea how the two could be combined, but I sensed that if they could form a dialogue the result would be a very unique book – something that stepped outside of the cage of genre. The more I thought about the poetry and prose mixture in a book, the more I kept asking myself, "What does this remind me of?"

The autumn prior to Michael's suggestion, I had co-ordinated a conference in Barrie on James Reaney with Tom Gerry of Laurentian University. One of Reaney's books that fascinated me was *Twelve Letters to a Small Town*. Reaney had explained during an interview Brian O'Riordan and I did (the interview appeared in *In Their Words*) that *Twelve Letters* was "an emblem book." My sister, Dr. Carolyn Meyer, had purchased an early eighteenth-century emblem book in England during one of our visits there because a professor of ours, David Hoenigger, had made an aside during a graduate tutorial about the lost tradition of works known as *emblemata*.

Emblem books emerged as popular works of literature in the early Renaissance. They featured elaborate woodcuts that illustrated a topic. The visual illustration was accompanied first by a poem so that the idea being presented could be remembered and absorbed, and then by a prose discussion of the visual's meaning. The combination of idea, picture, poem, and discussion transformed the image into a symbol by adding layers of ideas to it. The result was a book that was highly didactic but in a very simple and direct way (and didacticism in poetry has always been a major taboo in twentieth-century verse and, therefore, something that really needed to be put to the test and challenged, if only for the sake of art), and a book that made learning into an entertaining experience – the early version of edutainment.

I was still haunted by the fact that the emblem book was something I had experienced personally, and not just something I had puzzled over at the sill of my sister's bookcase. "Where had I seen this before," I kept asking myself. The answer came to me when I was helping my daughter sort out the volumes on the bookcase in her room when we were tidying up for the arrival of company. I came across a book that she had owned when she was a baby – she had eaten the first book we gave her when she teethed on it. Each of the cardboard pages contained a picture of an animal, and the animal's name boldly printed in bright block capitals beneath it. I have vague memories of such an animal book residing, and eventually disintegrating, on the table of my high chair. I looked at the contents page of Taj's manuscript that I had studied and toted all over Ontario for several months. Each animal represented a different letter of the alphabet. The animals lived not only in nature, but in the most basic structure of written language, the alphabet.

I telephone Michael. "Would you be interested in an emblem book? A book with the poetry portion by Taj, with the discursive portion by me, that is about animals? For example, A is for Ant, B is for Bee, etc.?" There was a moment of silence on the other end of the phone.

"I had a book just like that when I was child," Michael replied. "I think that was my first book. Just about everyone I know had a book like that."

That is how *Alphabestiary* came into being. That two individuals from very different cultures and hemispheres should meet because they both share a love of poetry, language, animals, and ideas is not a great wonder in this day and age. We live on a very small planet where someone in Mumbai can write and exchange ideas almost instantaneously with someone in Toronto. That world is growing smaller by the day with every pulse of a fibre optic cable or the beat of a satellite transmission. What makes the world small is not only that we share the same space and express the same ideas, but that we react in our own unique ways to what we encounter. It is essential that we share those reactions with one another.

The prose pieces in this book are not commentaries on Taj's profound and moving poems, but reactions, responses, reverberations, and resonances to the animals at the heart of each poem. In that sense, what I have to say about each animal is a translation of what Taj has said – I realize that each exegesis is often saying the same thing as his poem but in a different way. This is what resides at the heart of translation where the voice of the other "interprets the significance of what is said," and "moves or changes something from one place to another." The great struggle that confronts us in the world today is the struggle to translate ourselves to others, to make East intelligible to West and West intelligible to East without killing each other and every living thing that stands between us in the process. That is proving to be more and more an imperative in a small world. And yet, for the very smallness of the world we also have to acknowledge the nearness of other creatures and in our own ways celebrate them as gently and kindly and honourably as we possibly can. That's where the imaginative power of literature comes into play. I would rather look at an animal that is free in my mind than at an animal that is caged for observation. I would rather try to understand what someone else is thinking than to turn my back on them and refuse any attempt to bridge the silence between us. Living in this world should lead us to a celebration of each other rather than a denial.

When I was a child, one of the hymns I sang at Sunday School was "All Things Bright and Beautiful." It was written by David Livingston. My grandmother taught it to me because some distant relative on my grandfather's side had worked with Livingston in Africa. The hymn speaks of the fact that "all creatures great and small" were made by the same divinity that seems to vitalize and animate all living things – "each little flower that opens, each little bird that sings" – and it is in the spirit of that boundless animating energy, that force that inhabits the core of our language and our ability to communicate with each other, that I dare to celebrate the unique and irreplaceable individuality of myself, my fellow poet, and all living things.

Bruce Meyer, June 2011

An Introduction by H. Masud Taj

On the stage of the National Gallery of Canada, in front of a packed auditorium, my conversation with Arthur Erickson takes an unexpected turn. Erickson recalls growing up in Vancouver and embarking every weekend on nature trails: "We had a grandmother... she had this wonderful zest for life and she went so far as to say if I am reborn I would like to be reborn as a native because I think they are the only ones that understood the landscape."

I can't help but ask this doyen of Canadian architecture: "What would you like to be reborn as?"

He falls silent and then says, "Oh, I don't want to say an elephant — but they do get their own way." When the laughter dies down, I recite to him my "Elephant":

Inarticulate
Blob of ink;
Nose and tail
Out of scale,
Ears that would be
Wings.
White tusks precede
The body's darkness
Scanning eyes
Record the world.
Mind does not erase,
Does not overwrite;
Celebrates the excess
Of memory
With the memory
Of excess:

No bigness
Is big enough
When you have
Forgotten
How to forget.

"Elephant" had occurred in India[1], and here I was recalling it nine years later on the other side of the world. Perhaps elephants, with their proverbial memory, are ancestors of oral poets that forget to forget, and for whom poetry is part of everyday conversations, whether on stage or on the sidewalk.

While Erickson's grandmother took him on nature trails, my grandmother reminded me of the mother-tongue trail that went missing in my poetry. My poetry is in English, while an ancestor of mine was the classical Urdu poet whom a Harvard professor had referred to as "the high-sounding Amir Minai (1828-1900) who continued the Lucknow tradition."[2] Apart from his collected poems[3] and his later love lyrics,[4] Amir Minai was famous for his dictionary which remained incomplete thanks to his inexhaustible erudition.[5] In 1873, Amir Minai published an anthology of over four hundred Urdu poets[6] all of whom resided in a city smaller than contemporary Ottawa. Amir died in another centre of

---

[1] The poem was included in the solo exhibit at Galerie Jean Cocteau, "Downloading Animals: Oral Poetry & Calligraphy" Alliance Française de Bombay, 1999.

[2] Schimmel, Annemarie, *Classical Urdu Literature from the Beginning to Iqbal*. Wiesbaden: Horrassowitz., 1975. p.222. He went on to synthesize Lucknow's linguistic refinement with Delhi's spontaneity and was the last of the Urdu Formalists.

[3] *Diwan: Mirat al-ghaib*

[4] *Sanamhana-I ishq*

[5] He published two of the intended eight volumes of *Amir al-lughat*.

[6] *Intihab-I Yadgar* anthologizing 410 poets of Rampur, 1873.

Urdu literature in India, Hyderabad, where my wife Zeba was born and where we were married.

My mother, too, is an aficionado of Urdu fiction; her collection travels with her. All the books are inexplicably in the same untitled grey-green cover; she opens several before she finds the one she is looking for. Many of the novels have the last page or two in her own handwriting, not because the original went missing, but because she found the author's ending unsatisfactory. My father was an inspired Urdu poet for two memorable years of my childhood, turning our staid house into a tavern of *ghazal* guzzlers. I grew up with the elders at the dining table sprinkling their conversations with Urdu verses, even while having an argument. Even God chose to call his last bestseller *Recitation* (Quran), in which he claimed first and foremost to be All-Hearing as well as All-Seeing and All-Knowing. As a child, I learnt many of its haunting verses by heart.

So I thought poetry is something you do orally, and continued to compose poems in my head and leave them there: my oral poetry less the revival of an ancient tradition, and more a matter of personal accident. In an episode of the cartoon *Baby Huey*, a gangster duck challenges the big-hearted Huey by lifting him clean off the ground. Huey responds that even he can lift himself off the ground and proceeds to do that by levitating. The gangster duck rightly exclaims, "Hey! That's impossible! You can't do that," and Baby Huey's dad responds, "Hush! He doesn't know he can't." I too didn't know better, until it was too late and I found myself to be an oral poet (and also a calligrapher whose poetry paradoxically remained predominantly paper-phobic).

Along with my sisters Summi-the-storyteller and Noor-the-musician (apt company for a fledgling poet), I grew up in Bombay, now Mumbai. While the Quran had six of its chapters[7] named for animals – the Cow, the Cattle, the Bee, the Ant, the Spider and the Elephant – our home, by the Arabian Sea, was the inadvertent host to half of the animals (the smaller ones). We also welcomed, at one time or the other, several cats – a green-eyed black one that we were sure was a jinn; a cocker spaniel (in his own doghouse) with the incredibly soulful eyes of Michael Sarrazin; a variety of birds including an alcoholic hen (we suspect it was the gardener that kept her inebriated); a wounded black-shouldered kite that we nursed to health; white rabbits that rapidly multiplied confirming Abu Kamil's ninth-century breeding calculation (more commonly known as the Fibonacci series); fresh and salt-water fishes including a poisonous sea snake that the local fishermen called in their inimitable bilingualism *danger-machi* (fish); a head-bobbing lizard named Delilah with her two hatchlings; a baby octopus that didn't last too long; two turtles that almost lasted forever; and the invasion of large black mollusks each monsoon, ascending the white marble stairs of the house. Did not the Quran claim "There is not an animal (that lives) on the earth, nor a being that flies on its wings, but (forms part of) communities like you"?[8] In retrospect it appears, as ibn Arabi had asserted, we were needy of them more than they of us. Ibn Arabi's cosmology was structured by the twenty-eight letters of the Arabic alphabet, with the twenty-fifth letter being devoted to the world of animals, arguing, even in the twelfth century, for their rights.

Animals were virtual residents too, as we were honed in *hadith*: anecdotes from the life of the much documented Muhammad (p.b.o.h.), the prophet of Islam whose surname I thought was *Sallallahu'alaihiwasallam* as this was always pronounced after his name ("peace and blessings be upon him").

---

[7]Quran: chapters 2, 6, 16, 28, 29 and 105 respectively.
[8] Quran 6:38

His sayings and deeds were meticulously conveyed by a chain of narrators whom Muslims, in their vast corpus of theological writings in English, referred to as transmitters. (According to the Oxford Dictionary, a transmitter can be a person that transmits something from one person to another). One such transmitter was *Abu Hurairah*, literally "Father of Kitten," because of the kitten that always followed him. He reports how the Prophet once affirmed that a prostitute secured a place in heaven all because of a single instance when she fed water to a dog dying of thirst.[9] But there were many transmissions from the 'Dad of Kittens' that were anti-dog. The accomplished Islamic jurist and scholar, Khaled Abou El-Fadl, argues against them in his *tour de force* legal decision titled *Lord of Essence: Fatwa on Dogs*[10] leaving his own devotion to dogs intact.

When I turned thirteen, I began composing my poetry and have been at it since (I later learnt my ancestor Amir Minai began writing poems at the age of twelve, just as has my son has started doing now that he has passed his twelfth birthday). I was far from home in an enchanting boarding school named after its location high in the mist-laden mountains of southern India. The school was based on the atheist philosophy of the hyper-sceptic J. D. Krishnamurti. In his last journal he says,

> It is odd that we have so little relationship with nature, with the insects and the leaping frog and the owl that hoots among the hills calling for its mate. We never seem to have a feeling for all living things on the earth. If we could establish a deep abiding rela-

---

[9] *Sahih Bukhari*: Volume 4, Book 54, Number 538; Narrated by Abu Huraira.
[10] Abou El-Fadl, Khaled, *The Search for Beauty in Islam: A Conference of the Books* Lanham: Rowman & Littlefield, 2006, p.316.

tionship with nature we would never kill an animal for our appetite, we would never harm, vivisect, a monkey, a dog, a guinea pig for our benefit. We would find other ways to heal our wounds, heal our bodies. But the healing of the mind is something totally different. That healing gradually takes place if you are with nature, with that orange on the tree, and the blade of grass that pushes through the cement, and the hills covered, hidden, by the clouds.[11]

The school, hidden in a blue haze of eucalyptus trees by the clouds, was strictly vegetarian with unfertilized eggs being the only concession. We were introduced to the English translation of the *Panchatantra* in which animals spoke the Sanskrit *nitisastra* fables of third century BC, based on even more ancient oral traditions. The *Panchatantra* was India's first global bestseller, the precursor to the *Arabian Nights*, the European *Aesop's Fables*, and America's Disney. It was but natural that Mickey Mouse, Bugs Bunny, Tweety and Donald Duck should express themselves as humans. The 'P-fables' were structured as nested Russian dolls, with one story emboxed in another, and another, and another. Within a single story several other stories were told with characters sprouting epigrammatic verses much as the elders did at the dinner table. The tales vacillated from the Machiavellian to the eminently ethical and, as a lapsed vegan, I vacillated with them.

Little wonder at the name that Zeba and I chose for our son. If you ask him, "What is your name?" he will reply "Noah." But *"Tumhara naam kya hai?"* will elicit "Nuh." If *"Qu'est que c'est votre nom?"* is asked, then he will say

[11] Krishnamurti, J.D., *Krishnamurti to Himself*. Brockwood Park, Friday 25th February, 1983 www.jkrishnamurti.org

"Noé" sans h, while *"Ismak ay"* will evoke the mother-of-all-h "Nuh!" Noah, the floodrider's name, surfs the spectrum of languages. Soon after he was born, the poem "Dragonfly" occurred with its opening verse:

play time 2:25

> *My head is a conference of eyes*
> *I hold too many points of view*

opening the floodgates of animal poems and turning me into a one-man travelling zoo, reciting animals from memory to audiences in India, Europe and North America.

This selection in *Alphabestiary* is a cross-section of a rather voluminous virtual ark that floats across forgotten synapses. Bruce and I recited together at the cusp of the new millennium at the University of Toronto's Hart House Library Reading Series. When he saw the poems on the page a decade later, they immediately sparked off literary associations in his head. *Alphabestiary* was born at that instant. The title would come up later, during a conversation in a café. By then we had known each other for eleven years; one for each of his volumes that it was my good fortune to receive.

As in the ark, the animals come in pairs for a poet-calligrapher; the coupling of the oral-poem with its calligraphic counterpart (for the oral poet, paper is the convoluted folds of his twin hemispheres). When you listen to a poem the hearing in your inner ear occurs right next to the semi-circular canals, behind your eyes, that orient your body's balance. The reception of the oral poem remains visceral with your brain frantically trying to catch up with what the body has unwittingly responded to. In the case of its calligraphic representation, the form is the iconic signature of the aniconic. The book then is the zoomorphic aural-zoo unzipped; the typeset is the trace of the departed voice and calligraphy, and is ready to receive other voices and other forms.

One spring, eleven years after Noah's birth, our daughter was born. Noah named her Zahra in English, Zara in Spanish, Zaara in Hindi and Zahrah in Urdu and Arabic with the meaning migrating from "flower" to a "person of distinction" (i.e. the suffix of the Prophet's daughter). Both Noah/Noé/Nuh/Nuḥ and Zahra/Zara/Zaara/Zahrah encourage multiple readings depending on how they are enunciated. Enunciations harbour initiations: you breathe life into poems when you pronounce them. Contemporary singers[12] give voice to Amir's ghazal from another century: *sarakatii jaaye hai rukh se naqaab aahistaa-aahistaa / nikaltaa aa rahaa hai aaftaab aahistaa-aahistaa* where lifting the veil reveals the face, as slowly as the rising sun reveals itself and meaning dawns, slowly, very slowly.

play time 2:03

H. Masud Taj, May 2011

---

12 Jagjit Singh and Chitra, "*Golden Collection*," Vol. 1, Saregama, India, 1996.

ALPHABESTIARY

Ant

I do, therefore
Unmindfully, I am

A passing thought embodied.

A neuron on six neurotic feet
Crossing synapses in frenzy

Saying, "Read me! Read me!"

For I cannot read.
The sum total of all that I do

Is the thought that escapes me.

While I relentlessly fabricate
Mind, mindlessly.

Ants can ruin a picnic, yet the very systematic nature of how they behave is suggestive of the kind of church picnic behavior that Virgil tells us is what one does in Heaven or, at least, the Roman Fields of Elysium. They work very much as the harvesters work – they remind me of those bent-backed bodies stooped in the hot harvest sun above Holland Marsh on a hazy September afternoon. This sense of perpetual labour in the process of gathering may be why ants were associated with the grain goddess Ceres in the Classical European imagination, and were often used in auguring the future in much the same way that the modern stock market, the barometer of our labours in the world economy, is an indicator of the kind of short-term financial and even social future we all face. The great paradox in all this is that there is something extremely socialist about ants in that they remind me of a kind of utopian/dystopian sense of uniformity in action, a Marxian image of faceless masses that all move in step with one another. Those feelers on top of their heads are always searching for a connection to something individual that they never seem to find. To step on one, either purposely as children do or accidentally, is to remind us of our frailty, and, paradoxically, the loss of our own individuality.

Bull

My body is the sky at night

Tail is a flurry of comets
Trying to keep pace

Hoofs spew cosmic dust
Whirling into galaxies' swirls

The sliver of saliva
From the corner of my mouth
Is the strand of milky-way

The redness of my tongue
Is the falling in fleeting
Red-shifted stars

My bellow drowns the universe
Dies into a background noise
Of crackling radio waves

Nostrils are a flaring
Twin black hole system
Snorting last flares
Of collapsing suns

My eyes are a constellation of unborn stars

The crescent on my head
Is the first glimpse of an unravelling.

Who are you,
Standing with a shaft of light-years of light
And a flapping rag of warped space-time?

My movement in place
Towards you is all of creation.
The gravity between us
Is more than the universe can bear
As it flees from itself everywhere.

Bulls speak to us of an earthly strength, a practicality, and a profound sense of creative knowledge. That is why the constellation of Taurus, a star pattern in which the ancient Greeks saw the head of a bull, is associated with springtime, fertility, rebirth, and a powerfully majestic sense of male potency. The great paradox inherent in the bull is that while he is one of the twelve cornerstones of heaven, he is always associated with the earth – a connective figure that is divine in his ubiquity. His blood was considered sacred to ancient cults such as

Mithras because it was believed to be the ingredient that had to be shed in order for an individual to attain rebirth. The sacrificing of a bull, universally, is what seals a covenant or agreement between Heaven and Earth. God prefers Abel's blood offering on the pyre over Cain's burnt grain. Yet for all the connotations of rebirth that are associated with the bull, it is also linked to that haunting Western image of the god who must die every spring in order for the world to be reborn, both spiritually and vegetatively. The great medieval philosopher, Thomas Aquinas, lovingly accepted the nickname of "The Bull," as someone powerful enough in intellect to pull together the miasmas of Classical and Christian thought in his *Summa*. When the stout, bullish-looking professor died at Fossanova Abbey in 1274 while riding a donkey to Rome, the abbot of the monastery sold Aquinas' body piecemeal to raise funds for the religious house. All that remained of the great philosopher was his little finger. I am always reminded of Aquinas when a child asks me to give them a "pinky swear," the signing of covenant with innocence that I always feel obliged to uphold.

Cat

In the dreadful gleam of the cat's eyes:
The world at night is alight
With neon signs of life.

Goldfish are glowing lanterns underwater,
Angel fish are slivers of refracted moonbeams
Trapped in the cat's eyes,
Water's tensed skin is animated translite.

Fluorescent rats and mice are tight-fisted
Holographic knots with tails that twitch,
Or laser beams in full flight
They streak across the gulf
Between the cat's eyes.

Cats can see what bats cannot hear
As they hang from the tree:
Heartbeats of their upside-down hearts.
Infra-red stars twinkling
In the cats' night sky.

All that glows in the dark
Water, earth, sky
Are dying embers
For the cat that divides
Night world into categories of light,
And darkness defined by the coordinates
Of other cats' eyes.

Cats dream
With their eyes wide open
Pupils dilate to overtake the night.

Cats answer to no one. Folklore tells us that to look into a cat's eyes is to gaze into an eternal dark mystery that functions not according to the rules of the world, but to the call of its own nature. Cats have always been associated with dark magic, with the unseen, the unheard, and those inexplicable presences in nature that haunt us without speaking to us. The Egyptians believed they were creatures from the underworld. To cross the path of a black cat is to put oneself in the path of bad luck. The opening lines of Shakespeare's *Macbeth* reference a cat through the voice of the First Witch. As animals, cats are often associated with the Classical goddess of the hearth and home, Hecate, who was linked to witchcraft, crones, old women, and black magic with the coming of Christianity; yet the domesticity of the cat suggests that it is a creature that is symbolic of domestic security, a keeper of the house who protects food from rodents and whose presence is that of a comforter. Where the dark associations may have originated is in their taste for birds, winged creatures who are always associated with the soul. T.S. Eliot thought that cats had been given a bad rap by the Western imagination, and gave them lives and biographies in *Old Possum's Book of Practical Cats*. The ancient Egyptians understood the paradox that resides in cats: they perceive the cat as a symbol of the goddess Isis, the guardian of marriage. Good marriages are usually not far off the relationship between cat and master – each one goes their own way until someone needs to curl up, be rubbed the right way, or treated with warmth and affection. And each marriage functions not according to the rules of the world, but to the call of its own nature.

Dragon

I breathe in air, breathe out fire,
Reduce my mouth to cinders
Renew my tongue with each breath
My words are not felicitous
More corrosive than acid or fire.

To cope with dragon-reality
You conjure a white mythology
Of dragon-slayers.

No myth can last the cycle of my breath;
No fire in the breasts of your armoured knights
No glint of steel in their hand can withstand
The force of my breath, my acidic saliva,
The blaze in my eyes.

I am as large as memory
Whose dimensions none can encompass.
Doomed to an unforgiving unforgetting
I grow larger with time.

Between my sheer physicality
And, when I turn my back, my invisibility
I am half the phenomenon
You wish you could be
And I would die to be incomplete.

play time 4:22

44

Dragons owe a tremendous debt of gratitude to J.K. Rowling for their rehabilitation in contemporary literature. Dragons now possess associations with magic and wonder as part of a late twentieth-century fascination with dinosaurs. Give a child a plastic raptor and in ten minutes, with a healthy imagination, he'll have it flying. Traditionally, dragons – Tiamat in the ancient earth-mother cults, were symbolic of old pagan religions that preceded Christianity, and were always linked with evil, Satan, and the kind of abject terror that is interwoven in such monsters as Grendel's mother or the final horrific and thanatic creature that mortally wounds the protagonist of *Beowulf*. Rowling and contemporary readers may be subconsciously realizing that the dragon is symbolic of the old, pre-Christian feminine principle in nature-driven beliefs. Now that she is reborn into the Western imagination with the same force that she possesses in the Chinese and Eastern traditions, there is the sense that the fire she breathes is a form of enlightenment and not merely a way to defend herself from a Capodocian knight. In the story of St. George, a young knight from Capodocia slays a dragon who is besieging a city in Libya. In one version, as depicted on the English gold sovereign coin of the nineteenth century, St. George slays the dragon. This slain-dragon version is the one that most readers associate with the mythical creature, and is the one used by Edmund Spenser in Book I of *The Faerie Queene*. In Spenser's view, the dragon represents the evils of Catholicism and Papist countermoves against emerging Reformation Protestantism in England. In the other version of the St. George legend, he tames the dragon, and leads it back to the city on a chain, docile, innocent, and re-sworn as a protector of the people, especially children.

Elephant

Inarticulate
Blob of ink;
Nose and tail
Out of scale,
Ears that would be
Wings.
White tusks precede
The body's darkness
Scanning eyes
Record the world.
Mind does not erase,
Does not overwrite;
Celebrates the excess
Of memory
With the memory
Of excess:
No bigness
Is big enough
When you have
Forgotten
How to forget.

Elephants are nature's expression of epistemology. They never forget. But the question is, why should they remember, and if they remember then how do they do it? David Hume questioned the veracity of memory. He said that in order for us to remember ideas or events, they had to be filtered through layers of perception: seeing, previous knowledge, and imagination, before the memories ever stuck in our heads. Thomas Hobbes suggested that the longer we hold memories, the more "dimme" they become. There is nothing dim about an elephant. They are large and they loom large in our imaginations. They frightened Alexander the Great's conquering army on the banks of the Indus. When they crossed the Alps with Hannibal, they terrified the Roman army with their enormity. They were the epitome of what the European imagination considered to be the terror within the sense of the sublime. Yet for all the power that they express in their shape and their tough sandpaper skin, there is something frail about the elephant. Joseph Conrad attempted to expose the enormous absurdity and horror of the African ivory trade of the late nineteenth century in his novel *Heart of Darkness*, and in doing so revealed something horrifying and enormous at the core of the European imagination – that atrocities could be committed for the sake of piano keys. For all the efforts that late twentieth-century re-imaginings of elephants have brought about – the cute story of Dumbo or cloying songs such as "Baby Elephant Walk" – the truth is that the elephant is on the verge of extinction and must be preserved because it is the largest of all land mammals, and its absence would create an enormous hole in nature that our imaginations cannot fill. This is something to remember. This is something one cannot forget.

Firefly

I burn without passion
Glow without heat.
My fire is nostalgic;
Embers without oxygen.

Species are a ceaseless
Galaxy; we are earthbound
Stars that swirl a cosmogony
And ignore the fixed

Cosmology of monsters
That feast upon themselves
Radiate heat
Fade into gaps in the sky.

My light is cold.
It is sheer intellect
And strategy:
I move, I mate,

Pass the torch,
I die and remain
Forever
Aflame.

Fireflies are the insect world's answer to the human abstraction of hope. They are the light in darkness, a statement of divinity in a minute form. One of the stained-glass windows in my old college portrayed the essayist and scientist Francis Bacon, and bore the motto "God shewes himself best in his smallest things." To see fireflies in action, to watch their blinking signals of unbridled will to life floating through the darkness on a humid summer night is to witness a miracle in nature that brings the stars down to earth. The element of fire suggests not only something hot and dry (and therefore able to rise to heaven) but also something that expresses the elemental passion that resides in all living things. In short, fire rhymes with desire because it is essentially the same thing. The firefly creates its light as both a display to impress its mate and to reveal itself to others. When I was about thirteen and just beginning to think about sex and the way the world keeps itself going through the power of passion, I found myself on Cape Cod one night surrounded by a myriad of fireflies. It was the first time I had experienced the wonder of the lights appearing and disappearing around me. I captured one in a glass jar and brought it into the cottage in the hope that it would glow in the night as I lay in bed. It did not. Once it was taken out of its place, its light went out. It had no one to speak to, and I believe it died of loneliness or from its inability to serve the purpose for which it was created – to share the divinity of its flame of desire with other fireflies who understood what it was trying to say in the darkness. Language gives us hope only when we understand it and are able to reply to those who speak to us.

Grasshopper

Nose and tongue are synonyms.
Restless antennas scan the sky.
I smell to taste,
Taste to smell.

Jaws are antonyms
At right angles.
Front chops up and down,
Rear grinds side to side.

Ears are stomach-bound
To digest sound.
The sound I make with my feet
Is no food for your thought.

Map your senses
On to my frame of reference,
Your thighs will bulge
With muscular insights.

You will witness
The world the way I do,
Take a leap of faith,
Fly.

Grasshoppers are nature's way of reminding us of the existence of time and space, and that we exist in time and space. According to Ovid, Tithonus was granted eternal life but not eternal youth and, as is the case with many such characters who are cursed with everlasting life but with no other conditions or limitations (Sibyl, for example), Tithonus shrivels and turns into a grasshopper. In the Anglo-Saxon world, the word "wandære" meant both a wanderer and a grasshopper or "treader of the earth." In "The Wanderer," a displaced, exiled and homeless man recalls the world that he has lost, the society that crumbled around him, and the lovelessness of the world. Locusts that destroy crops are essentially large grasshoppers that appear in clouds and ravage everything in their path with their ravenous hunger. As symbols of hunger, false or destructive harvests, or simply aging, grasshoppers play their most noticeable roles in nature in the late summer and early September and are, in North America, harbingers of winter with whom farmers must struggle for their share of the crop. When I was in Grade Two, the first poem (and I have never found out who wrote it despite many searches) I memorized was "September:" "A road like brown ribbon / A sky that is blue / A forest of green / With the sun peeping through. / Asters deep purple / A grasshopper's call, / Today it is summer / Tomorrow it is fall." Each time one leaps from the long, dry grass in the park near my home, I think of the grasshopper as a bell, sounding the end of another year.

Horse

My body is all gravity,
My ankles all grace.
My skin is a seismograph:
Shock-waves
Ripple beneath the sheen;
Earth tremors that connect
Shiva's shoulders with Parvati's shanks
The rest of me copes with my androgyny.

My movement is meditation.
Canter is mere foreplay,
When I break into a gallop
The circle of horizon
Begins to slip away,
As I touch down to beat
The world with my feet
So that it may spin.

My eyes are twin holes;
My eyelashes: scorched rays
Of light that could not flee.
At the twitch of my nostrils
Stars flicker away.
Each time I turn my head
Swirling my mane, spiraling off galaxies,
I watch the universe change.

Horses run with tremendous power, and when their hooves touch the ground as they gallop and their manes fly with almost a wave-spray quality, I am reminded that they were associated with the sea god, Poseidon. The last lines of the *Iliad* tell us that Troy was not only duped by the gift of a large wooden horse, but was also the centre for horse worship and horse-breaking: "And the Trojans buried Hector, the breaker of horses." To be a "breaker of horses," not just a horse whisperer, was to possess the ability to harness unlimited natural energy, the energy of the sea. My father used to sit on the beach at Cape Cod and work out calculations with his slide rule and conclude that anyone who could capture the energy of the tides and the waves could answer the world's energy demands. The whitecaps come to mind. Throughout European folklore, the magical appearance of a white horse or horse-like spirit was read as a harbinger of death. In Charlotte Bronte's *Jane Eyre*, the protagonist is introduced to Mr. Rochester when he appears on a ghostly black horse that she mistakes for a phantom of the moors. Yet for all the dark connotations of the horse, what cannot be denied is that they are one of the most beautiful creatures in the world and are symbolic of the power of freedom. In South American film, the white horse is a code for revolution, for the desire to overpower order and install a new system of beliefs or understanding. Perhaps that is why the Romans (along with James Thurber's rendering for a Chicago-based poetry magazine simply titled *Poetry*) took the heroic ride of the hero Bellerophon on Pegasus as the emblem of poetry and poetic flight. The early Christians made a similar association with the horse and used it as a marker for St. Paul who concluded his letter to Timothy with the lines "I have run the race, I have finished the course," making the horse the betting man's favourite.

Iguana

It took six days to make the world
Given six letters of iguana.

The island cannot withstand solitude
It also cannot withstand the iguana.

Whichever road you take
Iguana will cross your path.

You will not find the iguana in the labyrinth
You will find the labyrinth in the iguana

It knows when it is not looking at you
You are never free of the gaze of the iguana.

When you see your life scroll past your eyes
You are looking into the eyes of the iguana.

Iguanas are dinosaurs that have been scaled down for efficiency. We had one in my Grade Five classroom. We were told never to let it catch cold because iguanas are susceptible to drafts, particularly in Canada. It was grey-green, with a long tail, and had yellow eyes with very small pupils that would rotate and look just beyond me rather than at me. One weekend, it escaped into the hot, dry, climes of the heating system, and was never seen again. I came to associate the iguana with disappearance, with the ability to change the colour of its skin in order to meld into the environment. I imagine an aluminum duct-coloured lizard still haunting the respiratory system of my grade school, living its solitary life in the shadows, and waiting for the return of its larger brethren. The next time I came in contact with an iguana was on the island of St. Maarten, where a group of them were sunning themselves on the patio of an expensive resort our bus tour stopped at long enough for us to buy island crafts. When I asked if they were sunning themselves I was told that they hung out on the patio because it was surrounded with hibiscus bushes. Several were chewing on the bright pink and red flowers. I found this surprising when I read an article in *Scientific American* or *Discovery* that in the time of the dinosaurs there were no flowers, that the bright floral displays we associate with plant life were a phenomenon that nature had invented long after the iguana's great relatives had vanished from the planet; yet there they were, those strange surviving vestiges of a different world, sustaining themselves on the same beauty and abundance that we consume. The great paradox they suggest as creatures is that they are cold-blooded reptiles that cannot exist without the warmth of the sun to keep their bodies alive. They seemed like Canadian tourists.

Jellyfish

You dream of form:
I appear in water.
You dream of time:
I begin to pulsate.

You dream of life:
I, made in water,
Made of water,
Move in water.

(Somewhere, on land
There is a missing umbrella.
Somewhere, on land
You are drenched to your skin.

Somewhere, on land
You have given up searching
You have taken to dreaming.
Somewhere, on land,

Your missing umbrella
Is waiting for someone
Somewhere, on land,
To open its wings.)

Somewhere in the ocean
A portion of water
Is refracting light
In unseen ways.

*J*ellyfish are the sea's party joke. If they are small and transparent as a window and you look at them underwater, they resemble line-drawings against the green of the ocean. They move with a balletic grace that would make Diaghilev envy, and your imagination wants to colour them in, to give them substance as they move almost without knowing that they do as they seek their prey. When they are larger and appear above water, such as they do in the form of the Portuguese Man O'War, they lack the sense of self-direction and individual propulsion that makes their small varieties so interesting. The Man O'War is a jellyfish that is large and sail-shaped, and when they grow large they appear as bubbles or sailboats near the surface of the waves and are blown in whatever direction the wind takes them. Their stinging tentacles can grow up to thirty-feet long, and often break off and float like strands of fishing line with the tides. I swam into one when I was snorkeling one afternoon at Cape Cod. With the instantaneous, paralyzing sting, I twisted in the water and soon found that I did not know which way was up. I swam to what I thought was the surface and my diving mask came crashing off as I hit bottom twenty feet down. I started to drown and I had stopped swimming to pull the invisible stinging strand off my neck. I suddenly pushed off with my feet and shot to the surface like a cork. I was told, as I was treated for shock and for the venom, that the one thing one should always carry to the beach in case of an encounter with a Man O'War is Windex. The ammonia in it neutralizes the jellyfish's toxins.

Kangaroo

I am empty.
My two large feet
Carry my emptiness
With a spring in each step.

I travel light.
My travelling companion
Is also empty, carrying
Emptiness in my emptiness.

I pass on to my baby
The pleasures of front-packing
The passion for dispossession
The destiny of infinite regress.

Kangaroos are the national symbol of Australia. My first encounter with these creatures came when my mother gave me an old, oversized, Australian penny that had belonged to some Aussie children who lived up the street from her when she was a child. The obverse featured a kangaroo. At Expo 67, I stood in the Australian pavilion for over an hour waiting for a mother kangaroo to produce the joey from her pouch. Kangaroos are suggestive of aspirations. They are nature's idea of hope. Their powerful legs and their famous hop connote speed and an almost not too elusive dream of being able to fly. Their symbolic connection to the properties of lift and flight – almost as if they are constantly attempting to defy gravity – may have been what inspired my father, a medal-winning figure skater, to purchase a pair of kangaroo leather skates in the late 1930s. Whenever I see a kangaroo, I think of my father on his figure skates, the gracefulness of the way he flew across the ice, the spring in his steps and jumps, as if the ice were a blue sky and his arms had grown wings. The leather in the skates is still as supple and soft as a gentle, caring hand, yet as I press it between my fingers it still wants to spring back into its shape, still wanting to jump and fly.

Lion

What would I be
Without my roar?

Without my measured walk
My padded paws

My ruffled mane
My rippling skin

My surprising turn
My sweeping glance

That sees it all?
Were it to fall on you,

What would you be
Without my glance?

Lions are the royalty of animals. They represent light, not only in the zodiac sign of Leo (the symbol for which is a stylized lion head), but also the illumination that comes from courage. Lions possess religious significance in that winged versions are the old Christian symbol for the Gospel of Mark, the reportage gospel. A winged lion sits atop a column in the square outside St. Mark's Cathedral in Venice where Mark is the patron saint of the city. As in the case of the lion Aslan in C.S. Lewis' *The Lion, the Witch and the Wardrobe*, the lion is a messenger. In heraldry, he is reserved for royal lineage. When lions appear on national flags, such as the Shah of Iran's or Haile Selassie's from Ethiopia, it has a way of telling the rest of the world that an absolutist view of life, politics and government reign. The Canadian coat of arms bears a lion, but it also features a unicorn on the opposite side of the shield (unicorns are symbols of purity) to temper the raw, almost brute power of the lion with gracefulness. In Canada where there are no indigenous lions, the absolutist saying *Dieu et Mon Droit* is replaced by a gentler geographic observation, *Ad mare usque ad mare.* Dante perceived the lion as symbolic of pride when he noted that hell contained three key sins: the Leopard (Impulse), the Lion (Pride) and the Wolf (Plotting). The sense of pomp that resides in the lion also connotes a laziness (female lions do all the hunting and gathering of food) and the idea that other creatures have to obey what he says. Sir Edward Landseer's stone lions in London's Trafalgar Square were designed to communicate this sense of pomp and power in order to prove that the square was the centre of an empire on which the sun never set. Cue Elgar's "Pomp and Circumstance March, Number 1." Now, fluff your mane. You look lovely.

Mosquito

When I fly over
This land of earthquakes
I fly under radar, avoid caves
That conceal sonar detectors.

I can trace from above
Underground rivers.
I touch down softly amidst
Grass that grows far apart.

I salivate to freeze the ground
To stall seismic waves
That set off avalanches.
Only then do I penetrate,

There is no pleasure in life greater
Than forcing yourself into
Blue underground rivers
In which red rivers flow.

This land is the land
Of my ancestors,
But I am only stopping
For a refill.

Mosquitoes are the Sirens of summer. They hover in clouds over the lakes of Canada, lurk in the shades of evening patios, and seek to suck the life out of anyone they can find. That high-pitched whine that echoes in the dark and unnerves anyone with ears is like music. My wife and I once stopped at dusk at the French River Trading Post in Northern Ontario. I was slow getting into the car, and a cloud of mosquitoes, sensing the carbon dioxide my body gave off as a signal for live bait, followed me. By the time we got to Sudbury, we were covered in bites. We had slapped about sixty against the windows as we passed Britt and Alban. In the cool of the night, we opened the doors and they flew out into the darkness before we continued our drive. I put on Miles Davis's "Round Midnight." My wife pulled the car to the shoulder. "His trumpet!" she complained loudly. "It sounds like a mosquito." Not only can a mosquito ruin a summer evening, it can also ruin the music of the stars. There is a terrible, vampire quality to the insect in that the female's sole purpose for torturing human beings with the itchy welt left from the anesthetic it injects to draw blood is to remain undetected, stealthy, and larcenous. In recent years, the Canadian mosquito has been associated with the deadly West Nile virus, a disease that I experienced after a mosquito bite. It can paralyze a body. For me, it wiped out my short term memory for several months. They were winter months. By the time I remembered, the mosquitoes had returned for another year, clouds and clouds of them, a plague against the stars.

Newt

My body is the site
For your assault
For my vengeance,
Each cell reproduces
Revenge.
I pray, I pray
C'mon, c'mon
Make my day,

You hack away
My limbs, my tail, my tongue.
I, a manic obsessive,
Regenerate in a frenzy
My tongue, my tail, my limbs.
You gouge my eye
I hold your gaze
With the one that is left
While I regenerate the other
To see you anew.

My creation destroys
Your destruction.
You turn believer,
Believe that I am forever.
I have no use for your beliefs.
I am not forever,
I am merely forever complete.

Newts don't fare well in literature. One gets its eye tossed in a cauldron in the opening act of *Macbeth* in order to create a spell wherein the three witches can augur the future. As a member of the salamander family and an amphibian, the newt is said to be able to live in fire as well as its natural habitat of water, and, alas, many poor newts end up falling victim to legend. When perceived as a salamander, newts also carry the suggestion that they are able to adapt and transform themselves by changing their colour. They are the Benedict Arnolds of the animal world, which is not a great trait to have and an unfair tag to hang on such a small and fascinating little creature. In Northern Ontario's wet lands (call them swamps if you wish) there are creatures called Mudpuppies which are part of the same extended family of newts and salamanders and other soft-skinned amphibians that resemble reptiles. My wife used to play with mudpuppies when she was a child growing up in Elliot Lake. What is interesting to me about the entire family of newts and salamanders and mudpuppies is their antiquity and their frailty. They are now an endangered species. I remember an older cousin showing me one that he had in a margarine tub at his cottage up north. He had named it Sally. When he picked it up by its tail, the frightened creature attempted to free itself and severed its own appendage, or so I was told. I remember that my cousin looked ashamed and slightly frightened, and even though I told him that starfish do the same thing when they think they are captured, he remained unnerved by the experience. What newts tell us is that even in frailty, and in retreat from the overpowering presence of man, nature remains courageous and still finds a way to fight back.

Owl

I have my eyes on you
You dwell within my gaze
Live out your life until I blink.

You cannot see my eyes:
Holes too big for the sky.

Stars flicker and die
The fleeting universe finally
Halts and collapses.

I do not stir
Nothing has caught my attention
Yet.

Owls originally were birds of terror in the Western imagination, possibly because of their taste for carrion and small rodents. They are hard to find. Usually, the only traces they leave in daylight are the balls of mouse fur and undigested bones they cough up. The Egyptians associated their presence with death, possibly because they hunt for flesh by night. For that culture, the owl conveyed the ideas of night, cold, and paralysis. The Greeks perceived owls in a different light. In the *Odyssey*, Homer says that one of the avatars of Athena, goddess of wisdom and knowledge, is the owl. She perches on the spar of Odysseus' ship and acts as a guide for him and a protector against the other gods that would prevent him from reaching home. At the same time, Athena is Mentor to his son Telemachus, and instructs or mentors him in his search for his father. The ancient sculptor Phideas, who carved the gigantic statue of Athena in the Parthenon, placed an owl on her right shoulder, an act that suggests not only her patronage of the city that bears her name, but a prevailing spirit of good judgment. Owls have been traditionally associated with wisdom, in part largely because they see so well in the dark, can turn their heads more than three hundred degrees, and because the eyes are wide and round and possess a piercing gaze. Many years ago, I found a small, confused, grey barn owl perched in the lower bough of a tree in my backyard. Fearing that it might fall prey to a cat, I stayed with it for most of a rainy day. Its round yellow eyes looked not only at me but into me as if it was reading my soul. When it regained its strength, it flew away, leaving me the wiser for having stood by it. Many Renaissance artists used the owl to portray sleep, and, in fact, when I lay down that night and closed my eyes in the dark, I was certain I could see the owl.

Parrot

My tongue is your tongue,
I mimic the sounds you make.
In the sentences I emulate
I do not understand a word.
I make progress by reading
The expressions on your face.

I whistle when I wish to speak
What is really on my mind.
But of late, you have begun
To mimic my whistle-song.
Its form is music to your ears,
Its content is something else.

To be civilized is to be subtle,
To speak between the lines,
To curse in seductive ways.

Parrots are obsessions with wings because they repeat, over and over, whatever they hear. And it all depends on what they hear. They are often perceived, as birds are, as symbols of the soul. What parrots do, however, is remind us of what our souls are trying to tell us because they mirror and echo the mantras we utter to ourselves so often that we fail to listen to what comes from our own mouths. Julian Barnes uses a search for a taxidermied Amazonian parrot Flaubert studied while writing *Un Coeur Simple* in order to examine how we deflect grief through obsession. My grandmother used to tell me about a very strict Presbyterian minister she knew who purchased a parrot without knowing that it had belonged to a sea captain for most of its life. Whenever it swore and cussed, usually during teas the minister's wife gave for ladies of the Temperance League, the reverend would throw a black cloth over the bird's cage. Nevertheless, it would keep cussing, repeating over and over the same words that the minister deemed evil. Considering the bird to be the devil incarnate, the minister eventually took it down to Pier Four in the docks of Toronto where it became a popular and hilarious fixture among the stevedores well into the twentieth century. It never crossed the dock workers' minds that there was anything wrong with the bird. He spoke their language, and they were happy and reassured to see themselves mirrored in their feathered friend. Comedy, in its essence and its traditional origins, is all about looking in a mirror and seeing oneself reflected, exaggerated, and overblown to the point where we laugh at ourselves. Robert Louis Stevenson's classic character, Long John Silver, has a parrot perched on his shoulder wherever he goes because even pirates need company, and the best way to laugh is to be beside oneself with laughter.

Quail

Black head plume
Chi-CA-go
Black head
Chi-CA-go
White forehead
Chi-CA-go
Black bill
White-streaked throat
Chi-CA-go
Chi-CA-go
Grey feathers brown feathers
Streaked with white
Belly white belly brown
Chi-CA-go
Chi-CA-go
Chi-CA-go
Grey tail
Grey legs brown legs
Chi-CA-go
Chi-CA-go
Cream-coloured eggs
Chi-CA-go
With brown markings
Chi-CA-go
Wherever they hatch
Chi-CA-go
Where-chi-ever-CA-they-go
Chi-CA-go

Quails are treated like chickens, which is a great shame because they are not bred like chickens. Their eggs feature in numerous recipes. I wanted to see what a quail would look like when it dressed itself rather than being dressed by a chef, and most of the pictures I have seen of living quails remind me of the Ontario bobolink, a roundish bird that loves to live in tall scrub grass. I watched a covey of quails (note that they are spoken of in terms of collective nouns), or should I say a bevy of bobolinks from a friend's patio one spring day in the farm hills north of Cobourg. They struggle to become airborne because the ratio of wing to body is an aeronautical nightmare. As they take flight, they squeal and squeak as if to suggest enormous strain on their part. At a friend's dinner party one evening, the hostess put out a tray of tiny splayed bird bodies. My first reaction was, "Aw, not Tweety!" before she told me that they were quails. Still, I remembered holding my dying canary in my hands and feeling his heart beating down to its last count in his warm and tiny body. I did eat the quail, as I didn't want to insult the hostess. The flavour is slightly more sour and pungent than that of chicken, but what troubled me with each bite (and there weren't many bites on the quail) was their tininess, the frailty and delicacy of their bones. They were not food but small tragedies on a plate. I imagined that they had been picked off in a field of grass or wildflowers as they struggled to take flight, and had given themselves away with their straining cry. "No," the hostess said, "they are domestic, not wild, quails." The idea of a hand reaching into a bird cage flashed through my mind, and for the rest of the evening I felt very ashamed of myself, and wanted to apologize to the birds in the garden for what I had done.

Rat

I am not squirrel, not bat;
Not cute, not weird;
I am rat

My fingers are slender
My eyes are sharp
My teeth can pierce
Your thoughts because

I dwell in the dwelling
Of your thinking
That divides the world
Into two traps:
Rat / Non-Rat.

Being the way you think:
I am unthinkable.

Rats are what they are, but as they are they are a creature that has acquired a great deal of symbolic baggage because of what we have read into them. Rodents, by virtue of their scavenger tendencies, follow sources of food – primarily what is left behind by human beings. The rat has always been identified with death, decay, decomposition, and with cowardice. These associations came long before it was discovered that they were the carriers of the Bubonic Plague that wiped out almost two thirds of Europe's population during the thirteenth century. As the corpses, or "rosies," exploded from the toxic gases given off by the pustules and swollen limbs of the afflicted, mourners would hold "a pocket full of posies" or a nosegay to their nostrils to mitigate the scent of death. The children's rhyme "Ring-around-a-rosy" is our dark reminder of the great fear of the Black Death and its unknown causes. Strangely enough, the gene that enabled the remaining one third of Europe to survive the viral slaughter is the same gene that today triggers Alzheimer's disease in the descendants of the plague's survivors. One Medieval saint, St. Fina, is associated with rats because she lived in a garret filled with them and gave herself to a life of poverty. In all likelihood, as she lived during the time of the Plague, she probably possessed the gene that immunized her against the bites of fleas that were carried by rats. Regardless of saints, the rat is still perceived as a very self-absorbed and self-preserving creature – the ego we hide beneath our layers of civilized decorum – and be the first to jump from a sinking ship, betray a friend or loyalty (as in "to rat out" someone), or be studied and tested to death in a laboratory. They are what they are, but for the purpose of science they are the one creature considered expendable that is most like us genetically.

Sheep

When my body appears
Hungry
The world divides into two
The part that I can eat
The part that is inedible.

The inedible world is irrelevant
The irrelevant world disappears
The remaining edible world divides
Into a world in close proximity
And a world held at a distance.

The distant world is irrelevant
The irrelevant world disappears
The remaining world near me divides
Into a world being erased as I eat
And the world that waits my eating.

Finally when all that is world
Is completely within me,
Within me the world divides
Into the relevant that diversifies
And the homogenous that is turd.

The world as turd is irrelevant
The irrelevant world disappears
Disappears too the relevant world
Into ovine blood, flesh and bones.
All that was world has turned into I.

And then, only then, my hunger abates
Then returns the homogenous turd,
Undifferentiated space, undivided world
And returns my undivided mind,
While my fulfilled body disappears.

Sheep are sponges for the wrongs of the world. Unlike goats which often take the blame for misdeeds or take the punishment (a scapegoat), sheep are surrogates for us that, because of their docile nature, stand between us and danger as protectors. Metaphorically, they free us from the world. They take away the sins of the world. They wait placidly in fields, grazing and minding their own business until someone paints a door frame with their blood as in the Book of Exodus, or sacrifices one in a offering of appeasement and supplication for forgiveness – whether it is caught by its horns in a thicket (Genesis) or nailed to the Tree of Knowledge in an act of Man's terrible inhumanity to Man (Gospel of John). What the

lamb takes into itself and seems to absorb like a round, white sponge is our own lack of animal respect for each other and the world we live in, the stuff of Sin. Placid in their white wool that almost seems to shine against green fields on a summer day, they suggest a peacefulness and orderliness to the world. Bach's "Sheep May Safely Graze" where the flocks are in their pastures, green, abiding, suggests that the sheep's sense of togetherness points us to a lost, elegiac, pastoral place where we were once orderly, peaceful, and at peace with ourselves. Sheep are always associated with The Golden Age in the Classical world. Counting sheep will put us to sleep which suggests they are guides to the inner peace that the distracting world will not let us find until we are ready to let go of the frenzy of conscious life. And just before we fall asleep, there is that moment when the wrongs of the world seem far away, so far, in fact, that we lose count of the number of sheep we see, and free of all the hubbub, permit ourselves a sojourn from this world.

Tiger

Do not take my name by day
Because I always hear my name
And then I turn to the one who calls
A fleeting glimpse and your heart will stall
Do not take my name by day.

Do not take my name at night
Because I always hear my name
And then I turn to the one who calls
He goes up in flames as my glance falls
Do not take my name at night.

Do not take my name at all
Because I always hear my name
And then I turn to the one who calls
Absorbing the caller erasing the call
Do not take my name at all.

Do not take my name by day
Do not take my name at night
Do not take my name at all
Because I always hear my name
And then I turn to the one who calls.

Tigers in the Western tradition are associated with wrath, cruelty and the world of harsh realities. It is hard for anyone to say anything about a tiger and not echo William Blake in his poem from *Songs of Innocence and Experience*. Blake suggested that the 'tyger' is "burning bright" in "the forests of the night," and that there is something uncontainable about the large cat. Their reputation for fearsomeness in the West has been exploited by circuses. I saw my first tiger when I was taken to Barnum and Bailey's Circus at Maple Leaf Gardens when I was five. My mother, rightly so, did not believe in animal circuses. She felt the animals were being exploited. The lion-tamer and tiger-master made the felines stand ridiculously on brightly painted pedestals. He snapped his whip at them as they pawed the air and bared their ferocious teeth. They were meant to thrill the audience with the raw power of the sublime that Blake sought to capture in his poem. On the way out of the Gardens, the father of the friend who brought me to the circus took a shortcut to his car that was parked behind the arena (he had pull with some of the big-wigs). We walked down a narrow corridor that was meant only for the circus workers, and there, in the stench of the hallway, was a large tiger. The friend's mother pulled me back as I approached the cage, thinking that I would be eaten alive and she would have to explain the grisly truth to my parents, but the cat was docile. It lay stretched out, exhausted and humiliated on the floor of the cage, and as I passed it gave me a look I have seen in the faces of humans when they are defeated, and it peered through the bars of its wheeled enclosure and heaved with what can only be a sigh as it looked at the world through the harsh reality of its cage bars.

Umbrellabird

I spiral around a vertical axis

Live in the lowlands
At the mountain foothills
Breed near the peak
High above the clouds

Reproducing another
Axial migrant
With a tuft of black
Forward facing feathers

And an altitudinal attitude.

Umbrellabirds are crows that have been dressed up in black hats. When I was spending my summers on Cape Cod as a child, I remember being told about widows' walks, those railed platforms atop New England sea captains' houses. Those perches were intended for the wives of the captains as places where the women could watch, a la *Tristan and Iseult*, for the return of their husbands from sea. In actuality, those walks are nothing more than an adornment of Federalist architectural style, but as a child I got the story confused. I pointed one out to my grandmother and told her that the high decks on the houses were places where widows went to look for captains they could marry. I could imagine the widow done up in her black weeds, her bonnet prominent atop her nineteenth-century head, and her dark dress publically advertising her eligibility. That's a long way around to saying what umbrellabirds remind me of. I carry a black umbrella whenever I go out. One of the first times I kissed my wife, I had that same umbrella up against a soft, wet snowfall as we kissed beneath it on Avenue Road. It strikes me now that the umbrella that the bird wears is much like the one we kissed beneath, and although the umbrellabird is native to the Amazon (and I have never been up the Amazon), the very fact that there are still umbrellabirds tells me that love is universal and unending, and that no matter who or what we are, we all need love to survive...even the widows and the sea captains.

Viper

My eyes can see
What you can only feel.
Long leisurely infrared wave
To you is heat
To me is sight.

I can see you at night
Your body heat gives you away
Betrayal at 98.6 degrees Fahrenheit.

At night the desert blooms
Into a garden of earthly delights
A gourmet's paradise,
Las Vegas of fast-food joints
Blazing neon, "This is I —
Fresh food with a perishable heart
Pulsating to keep my cadaver fresh
Dying to meet you!"
I eat my way into your afterlife.

I believe in a menu
That is an orgy of choices
From the micro-morsel
To the meat-monumental.

I believe in a consumer society.
For I am the consumer
You, the consumed.

Vipers or snakes are nature's enigmas of change and because we fail to understand them, as we should, we fear them, shun them, and mistreat them. When the serpent tempts Eve in Christian mythology, he is punished by God by being demonized for what is essentially a human failing. He is told that he will be crushed under foot and be vilified by all humanity. Being an outsider is not a good deal. According to Medieval legends and even Michelangelo, the snake originally had arms and legs. He is depicted in one of the panels of the ceiling of the Sistine Chapel as a hybrid creature with the body of an iguana and the head of a woman. Before the fall of man, Michelangelo's 'subtil serpent' has blond hair. Eve has brown hair. After the fall, Eve's hair turns blond. She becomes the non-Italian, the Germanic barbarian, the outsider in the artist's little visual joke. But beyond Renaissance artistic comments, the serpent has always suggested a powerful energy of regeneration, perhaps because it sloughs off its skin. A serpent with a tail in its mouth, an *ouroboros*, represents eternity, the continual struggle between beginning and end, death and birth, and rebirth and death that never ceases. What tempted Eve in the Garden of Eden may not have just been Sin, but the understanding that Time must enter the world so that it can not only come to an inevitable end where Man returns to God, but where it has the chance to begin again and again, so that we should not fear regeneration of any kind. What entered the world with the Fall of Man was the realization that things are what they are, and that can be an extremely frightening idea when what one mistakes for happiness is nothing more than a blissful and bland eternity where nothing changes.

Whale

I am the ocean made flesh;
Formless congealed into form.

My eye encapsulates the sky;
Clouds are my changing moods.

I am substantial but subtle too;
I live my life in slow motion.

My breathing
Is a holding of breaths:

Take an age to submerge,
An epoch to re-emerge and exhale!

The world inhales
And changes into a different world

Under a sky
No longer blue.

Whales are one of the first creatures in the Bible to be mentioned by name (Gen 1:23 "And God created the great whales") because of their size, power, and the underlying sense that they are, like us, a warm-blooded mammal. Some versions of the Bible such as the Catholic Jerusalem Bible, however, change the word whale for "sea monster." I find that a shame. In later books of the Bible, the whale reappears as an instrument of God's will in the Book of Jonah, where to be in the belly of the whale is to be in hell or in a living death. Whales are also depicted as enormous presences that haunt the seas and fill the salt waters with the thanatic – Leviathan. Revelations says that at the end of time, Leviathan will be drawn out of the waters of the sea, the salt water, and "there shall be no more death." As archetypes of ambivalence, whales are good and evil embodied in one great being that is marvellous and terrifying, the essence of Western sublimity and divinity. Herman Melville, in an encyclopedic *tour de force*, summed up just about everything that can be said about great whales. They are the alpha and omega of living things, and as such are one of the most powerful expressions of the divine: the power in the universe that is both benign and destructive in the same breath.

I had a moment with a whale one day off Provincetown. The passengers on a whale watch had gone to the port side to observe a baleen sounding in the distance with a great spray with its v-shaped tail (a sign of victory) raised in the air. Alone on the starboard rail, a huge male from the pod rolled under the boat and floated with its left eye raised up from the water, staring into my eyes and studying me. It floated there for at least a minute, and in that minute I thought I had experienced a conversation with God, or at least the ultimate creation of all God's earthly wonders.

Xolo

If you do not believe
In blind faith:
Look into my eyes.

See yourself
Split into two
You belief in disbelief
Not exceeding my belief
In you.

But it is true
There is no blind faith
When there is no believer
When there is no belief
When there is you

Then both of you
Drown in my eyes
Drown belief and disbelief
Drown the skies
Drown all there is to be seen
Until there is nothing left to see

When there is nothing left to see
The eyes
Drown.

Xolos are hairless dogs. Dogs have always been associated with loyalty, with faithfulness, guardianship, and with the great virtue of commitment. Man's best friend has penetrated language and the imagination as few other creatures have. The order of Christian monks, the Dominicans, were not only named for St. Dominic – they were also a working pun on the Latin words "*domine*" or God and "*canes*" meaning dog. They were God's dogs, faithful followers always ready to serve and do the Lord's bidding in the world. Strangely enough, though it is of no real significance and only functions in English as an alphabetical fascination, dog is God spelled backwards. Lines and allusions about dogs appear at least five times in every Shakespeare play except *Pericles* – Shakespeare's most forgettable play – where the word or reference never appears. Shakespeare understood that the dog has a duplicitous nature. Homer suggested that dogs were harbingers of death and decay in his *Iliad*, the worldly manifestation of the harsh judgment and dismemberment that a soul would face in Hades. Later authors, such as Chaucer, revisited the dog as a symbol of wealth, prestige, and misplaced compassion. As Western literature evolved, so did the dog. The four-footed fur friend became a more familiar and kind creature. This evolution suggests that the dog is a reflection of our own natures, a barometer for how we are cared for and how we care for others and, as such, has evolved from the dark jackal Anubis of the Egyptian kingdom of death to become a mirror of our own enlightened and potentially caring souls. Maybe there is hope for us yet. Everyone, sit!

Yak

Long-haired,
Sure-footed,
Grazing on grass,
Browsing on herbs.

Swallowing,
Regurgitating,
Chewing,
Swallowing.

Weighing 2000 pounds;
Height: 2 metres;
Altitude: 20,000 feet;
Lifespan: only 20 winters.

Four part
Stomach
And only four
Quatrains.

Yaks are large, hairy, smelly bovine creatures, yet there is a mystical quality to them that reminds me of the Buddhist monks of their homeland. The first time I saw a yak was at Riverdale Zoo. None of the other children in my kindergarten class wanted to go near the creature because it was a hot day, the yak was ripe, and its heavy fur coat was swarming with flies. Yet in the yak's eyes, I saw something that spoke to me – a kind of patience and endurance, as if it was attempting to survive the humiliation of being caged while at the same time almost self-assured in what it told itself that it could outlast the heat, the noisy children, and the captivity. Its name has become a stand-in for pointless talking, yet the yak I encountered was silent and stoic. It met my gaze and we stared at each other. It is wrong to read human feelings into animals, wrong to personify them beyond what they are, but I came away with a respect for the yak, and I imagined what he would be like as he roamed the foothills and narrow passageways of the Himalayas. I wished him the silence of a cold mountainside, a fresh wind to carry the flies away. He stood there patiently in tune with his own rhythms, almost mindless to the world. I was just another demon he was turning away in his calm by refusing to acknowledge me beyond his penetrating stare.

Zebra

With all the sixteen million colours
I see the world in black and white.

I may have sixteen million strands of hair
But not a single one is out of place:
No white strand among the black
No black follicle among the white
This is the land of apartheid.

But when I move, my skin
Tells a different story:
Patterns swirl and mesmerize you
Do you see the white against the black?
Or black against the white?
Which is the figure; which is the ground?
I am the bipolar icon in black and white;
The black centre around which whiteness swirls
The white shroud concealed in darkness.

I have shattered the body's mirror-code
Set up a hypnotic complexity
Unravelled it all in black and white
And yet you do not decode.

Zebras, I was told as a child, are horses in striped pyjamas. They are the equine edition of a dichotomy because they are either black or white, though when one sees a living zebra it does possess that essential area of brown that suggests the possibility of compromise. To a zebra, the op-art of its stripes must be a form of beauty that attracts one zebra to another, so that what the zebra sees is not merely black and white, but the structure that forms unique and individual patterns. To see the world only in terms of black or white is a pity. The world cannot be defined merely as an either/or situation, east or west, but as a round orb that floats in infinite space and contains a myriad of possibilities. What I think the zebra teaches us is that what we possess in the way of our own unique patterns, and not merely the polarity of black versus white, is what allows us to speak to each other. One of the members of my ancestral family, Sir Isaac Newton, built a wheel on which he placed all the colours of the spectrum. When he spun the wheel, all the colours blended into white. The same principle of optics is true for patterns on a wheel. Look into the spokes of a hub cap in a car beside you as you head down the highway. The spokes will disappear, and you will see into the workings of the wheel, its brake drums, its axle joints, and remember that the world is also turning, so fast, that everything has the potential to become either one colour or to become transparent so that we can see into its workings. The great question I have heard philosophers ask about zebras is: "Are they white on black or are they black on white?" What really matters is that zebras, when they run, are charged with the freedom that horses also possess, the freedom of wind and space and speed that can carry them anywhere.

ACKNOWLEDGEMENTS

Thanks to Poetry Circle, Bombay, in whose volatile gatherings the animal poems stood their ground. Thanks in particular to its treasurer-poet Jerry Pinto for his feedback in the initial years. Thanks to poet-editor Ranjit Hoskote for including "Dragonfly" in his Penguin Book 2002 anthology: *Reasons for Belonging: Fourteen Contemporary Indian Poets*; to poet-editor Jeet Thayil for including "Cockroach" in his hefty anthology of 60 Indian poets (Fulcrum USA 2005, Bloodaxe UK 2008, Penguin India 2008); poet-editor Sudeep Sen for including "Tiger" in *The Literary Review* (USA 2009) and "Ant," "Horse" and "Jellyfish" in the forthcoming *Harper Collins* anthology; to Bina Sarkar, editor of the impeccable *International Gallerie*, who was in the audience at Alliance Francaise de Bombay in 1998 that featured 33 animals (until then) recited from memory and who a decade later requested "Bull," "Lion," "Sheep" and "Tiger" for the artist monograph that Bruce saw.

We are grateful to Sean Moreland for his feedback and advice on the manuscript as the book was taking shape. Thanks to Ted Fullerton of the School of Design and Visual Art at Georgian College for his suggestions about possible cover artists, and to Jon Merchant whose painting graces the cover. We would also like to thank the following people for their support of this book: Onnalee Groves and Rudi Quammie Williams of the City of Barrie Department of Culture; Melissa Robertson and Carolyn Bell Farrell of the Maclaren Art Centre in Barrie; Geoffrey Taylor of Harbourfront; John Degen of the Ontario Arts Council for his support of Bruce Meyer's work and encouragement of the collaborative process; Nina Callaghan for her keen eye; Barry Callaghan for his suggestions in the realm of prose; and Michael Callaghan of Exile Editions for believing in this project and its playful possibilities. Several of the poems and prose pieces in this book have also appeared in *ELQ* (*Exile: The Literary Quarterly*) Issue 35.3. We owe a special thank you to our families, and to all the animals, insects, beasties, and fowl.

About the Authors

H. Masud Taj is an oral poet, calligrapher, and architect who composes poems in his head and leaves them there. His downloaded poems have been featured in anthologies of Indian poets (*Penguin Books* India 2002; *Wespennest* Austria 2006; *Bloodaxe* UK 2008; *TLR* USA 2009) as well as Canadian poets (*Atlas* 2007; *Rogue Stimulus* 2010), and are archived in the *Special Poetry Collection* of Carleton University, where he is Adjunct Professor of Architecture. He was nominated for the best lecturer in TV Ontario's *Big Ideas* series in 2005 and is winner of the Capital Educator's Award for 2011. He lives with his family in Ottawa.

Bruce Meyer is author of 31 books of poetry, fiction, non-fiction, pedagogy and literary journalism including the national bestseller, *The Golden Thread*. With Barry Callaghan, he co-edited *We Wasn't Pals: Canadian Poetry and Prose of the First World War*. His broadcasts, *The Great Books, A Novel Idea*, and *Great Poetry* for CBC Radio One are the network's bestselling spoken word CD series. He is the inaugural Poet Laureate of the City of Barrie and Professor of English at Georgian College. He was named one of the ten best lecturers in TV Ontario's *Big Ideas* series in 2010. He lives with his family in Barrie, Ontario.

About the Cover Artist

Jonathan Merchant lives and works passionately as an artist. He has graduated from the Fine Arts Advanced program at Georgian College in Barrie, Ontario, where he has resided most of his life. Rewarded with the Queen Elizabeth II Aiming for the Top scholarship, and Barrie Art Club award, he will continue his education towards a Bachelor of Fine Arts while exhibiting his art whenever possible.